Girls Belong Everywhere

الفتيات ينتمين إلى كل مكان

By Kym Simoncini

Illustrated by Clarice Masajo

Please note, the two versions of this story have been written to be as close as possible. However, in some cases they differ to accommodate the nuances of each language.

برجاء ملاحظة أن نسختَي هذه القصة تمت كتابتهما لتكونا متقاربتين قدر الإمكان. لكن قد نكون هناك أحيانًا بعض الاختلافات لتناسب كل لغة.

Library For All Ltd.

Girls belong at school.

الفتيات ينتمين إلى المدرسة.

Girls belong at university.

الفتيات ينتمين إلى الجامعة.

Girls belong in hospitals.

الفتيات ينتمين إلى المستشفيات.

Girls belong in courts.

الفتيات ينتمين إلى قاعات المحاكم.

Girls belong in construction.

الفتيات ينتمين إلى مواقع البناء.

Girls belong in business.

الفتيات ينتمين إلى عالم الأعمال.

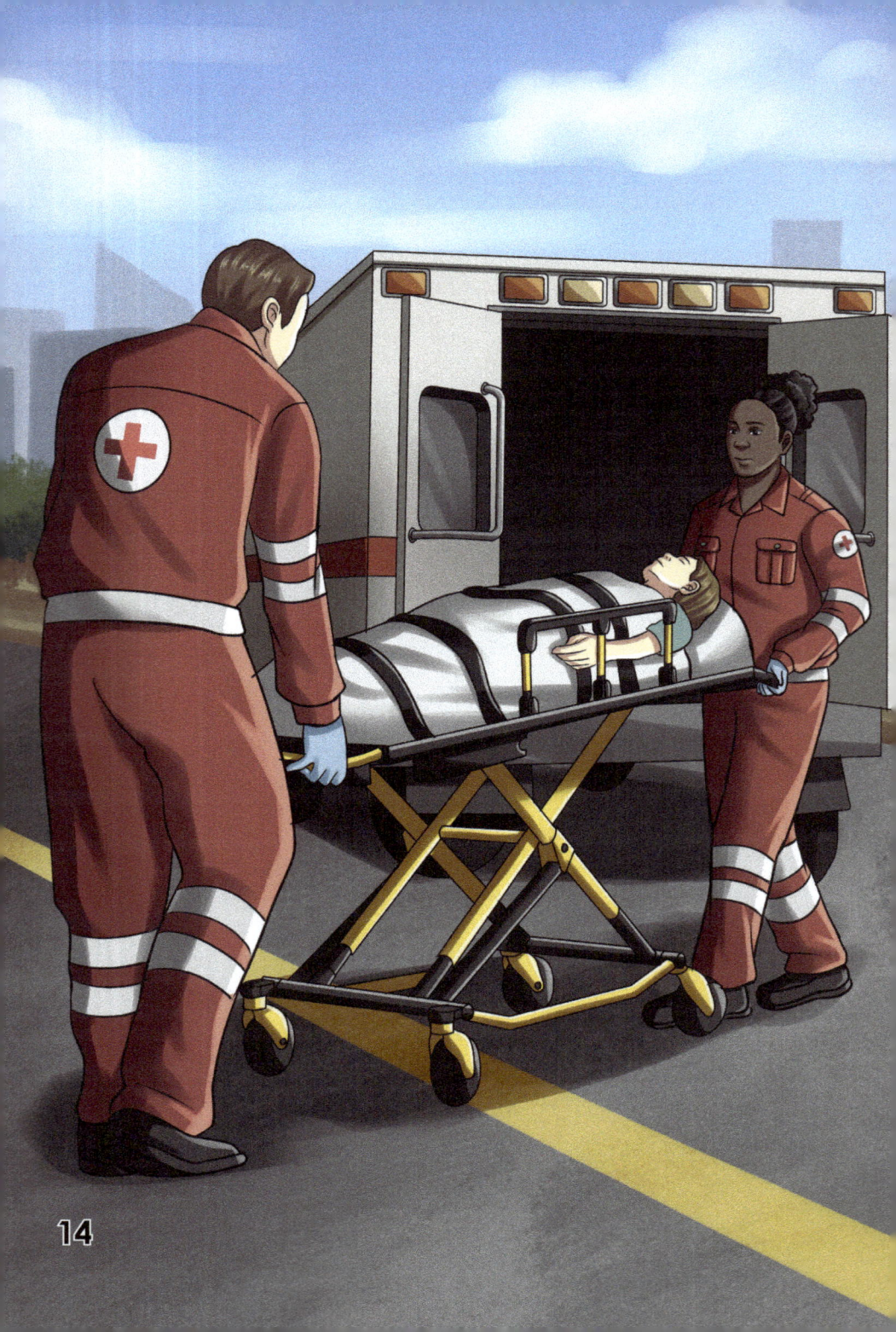

Girls belong in keeping the community safe.

الفتيات ينتمين إلى تأمين المجتمع.

Girls belong in the sky.

الفتيات ينتمين إلى السماء.

Girls belong on the sea.

الفتيات ينتمين إلى البحر.

Girls belong in the government.

الفتيات ينتمين إلى الحكومة.

Girls belong in laboratories.

الفتيات ينتمين إلى المعامل.

Girls belong in sports.

الفتيات ينتمين إلى الرياضة.

Girls belong in the arts.

الفتيات ينتمين إلى الفنون.

Girls belong in homes.

الفتيات ينتمين إلى المنازل.

Girls belong everywhere they want to be.

الفتيات ينتمين إلى أي مكان يرغبن في التواجد به.

You can use these questions to talk about this book with your family, friends and teachers.

What did you learn from this book?

Describe this book in one word. Funny? Scary? Colourful? Interesting?

How did this book make you feel when you finished reading it?

What was your favourite part of this book?

About the author

Kym Simoncini is an Associate Professor of Early Childhood and Primary Education at the University of Canberra, Australia. Kym grew up in Cairns, Queensland and enjoys working in Papua New Guinea as it reminds her of her childhood. Kym loves reading and believes all children have the right to read culturally relevant books.

Did you enjoy this book?

We have hundreds more expertly curated original stories to choose from.

We work in partnership with authors, educators, cultural advisors, governments and NGOs to bring the joy of reading to children everywhere.

Did you know?

We create global impact in these fields by embracing the United Nations Sustainable Development Goals.

3 GOOD HEALTH AND WELL-BEING	4 QUALITY EDUCATION	5 GENDER EQUALITY
8 DECENT WORK AND ECONOMIC GROWTH	9 INDUSTRY, INNOVATION AND INFRASTRUCTURE	10 REDUCED INEQUALITIES	11 SUSTAINABLE CITIES AND COMMUNITIES
12 RESPONSIBLE CONSUMPTION AND PRODUCTION	13 CLIMATE ACTION	16 PEACE, JUSTICE AND STRONG INSTITUTIONS	17 PARTNERSHIPS FOR THE GOALS

libraryforall.org

Published by Library For All Ltd
Email: info@libraryforall.org
URL: libraryforall.org

Original illustrations by Clarice Masajo

Girls Belong Everywhere
Simoncini, Kym
ISBN: 978-1-923207-02-8
SKU04364

www.ingramcontent.com/pod-product-compliance
Lightning Source LLC
Chambersburg PA
CBHW042340040426
42448CB00019B/3353